"To all those who still dream with their eyes closed;

Keep dreaming…"

C.J. Baker

My Big Natural Hair

© 2017 C.J. Baker

Written by: C.J. Baker
Illustrated by: Jasmine Hatcher

ISBN-13: 978-0692936085
ISBN-10: 0692936084

All rights reserved. No part of this publication may be reproduced, distributed, or transmitted in any form or by any means, including photocopying, recording, or other electronic or mechanical methods, without the prior written permission of the publisher and/or author, except in the case of brief quotations embodied in critical reviews and certain other noncommercial uses permitted by copyright law. For permission requests, write to the publisher, at the address below.

TEN19 MEDIA GROUP

P.O. Box 4454 | Tampa, FL 33677

Printed in the United States of America

My Big Natural Hair

My Big Natural Hair

By: C.J. Baker

My name is Amara.

I have big, natural hair.

Guess what? I love my hair!

My hair is so beautiful, I never care when the neighbors stare.

Momma says, "Our natural hair is not a burden to bear, and our differences are things we should share."

So without losing the smile I wear, I cheer loudly for my big hair!

As I skip joyfully down the street, my big hair follows along to its own harmonious beat.

My natural hair is so unique.

Momma changes the style several times a week.

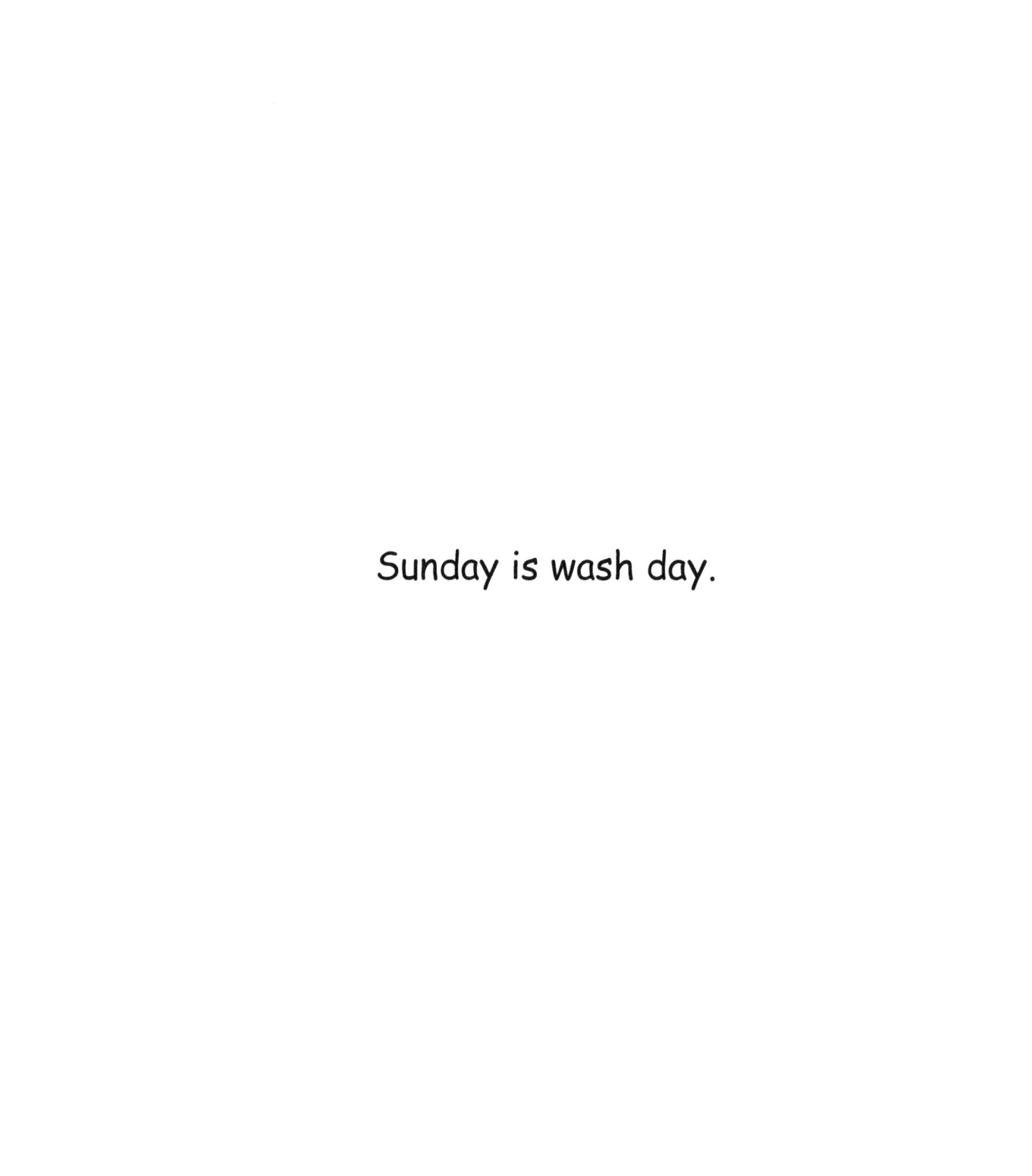

Sunday is wash day.

On Monday, I wear two afro puffs.

On Tuesday, I wear lots of braids.

On Wednesday, when I take my braids out, I have long crimped waves.

On Thursday, I wear pony tails.

On Friday, since the week is done, I wear one really big bun.

My hair and I have had such a busy week.

On Saturday, I take down my hair with ease.

Even our hair deserves to breathe.

My hair is magic.

My hair makes me feel free.

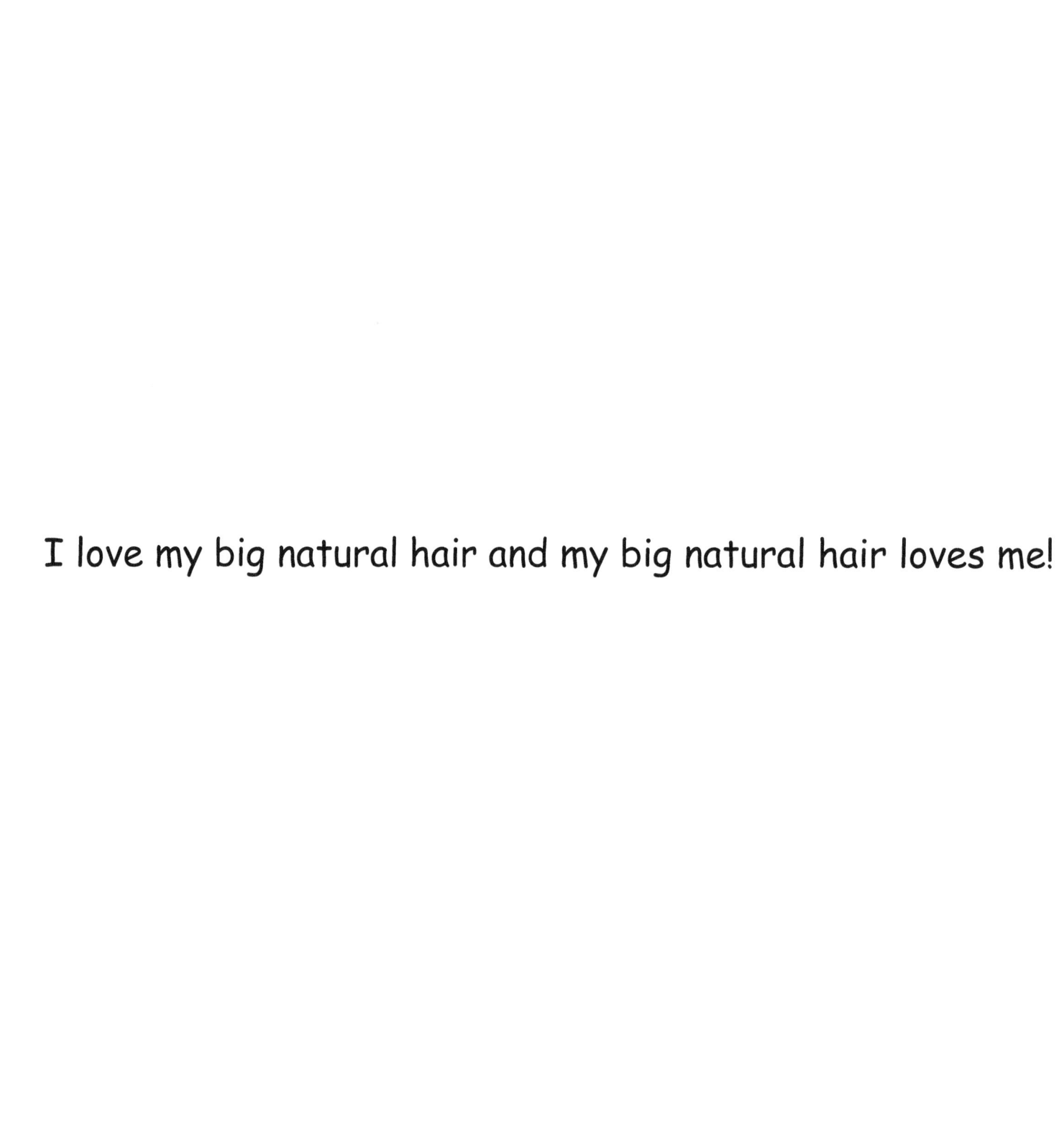

I love my big natural hair and my big natural hair loves me!

© 2017 C.J. Baker

www.ingramcontent.com/pod-product-compliance
Lightning Source LLC
Chambersburg PA
CBHW041536040426
42446CB00002B/113